Portfoolio 16

THE YEAR'S BEST CANADIAN EDITORIAL CARTOONS

EDITED BY GUY BADEAUX　　TEXT BY JAY STONE

M&S

© The Association of Canadian Editorial Cartoonists 2000
http://www.canadiancartoonists.com

All rights reserved. The use of any part of this publication reproduced,
transmitted in any form or by any means, electronic, mechanical, photocopying,
recording, or otherwise, or stored in a retrieval system, without the prior written
consent of the publisher – or, in case of photocopying or other reprographic
copying, a licence from the Canadian Copyright Licensing Agency –
is an infringement of the copyright law.

Canadian Cataloguing in Publication Data
The National Library of Canada has catalogued this publication as follows:
Main entry under title:
Portfoolio: Canada's best editorial cartoons

Annual.
Subtitle varies.
2000b   published by M&S.
ISSN 0839-6485
ISBN 0-7710-1051-6 (2000)

1. Canada - Politics and government - 1984-   - Caricatures and cartoons.*   2. World politics -
Caricatures and cartoons.   3. Canadian wit and humor, Pictorial.

NC1300.P67   971.064'7'0267   C89-030416-5

We acknowledge the financial support of the Government of Canada through
the Book Publishing Industry Development Program for our publishing activities.
We further acknowledge the support of the Canada Council for the Arts and
the Ontario Arts Council for our publishing program.

Edited by: **Guy Badeaux**
Text by: **Jay Stone**
Guy Badeaux is editorial cartoonist for *Le Droit* in Ottawa.
Jay Stone is the movie critic for the *Ottawa Citizen*.

Design by: **Mathilde Hébert**

Printed and bound in Canada

McClelland & Stewart Ltd.
The Canadian Publishers
481 University Ave.
Toronto, Ontario M5G 2E9
www.mcclelland.com

1 2 3 4 5   03 02 01 00

NATIONAL NEWSPAPER AWARD 1999

Raoul, 11 ans, comparaît devant la justice américaine pour inceste

GILDAS LE ROUX
AFP, GOLDEN, Colorado

Dix semaines après son arrestation, Raoul, un garçon américano-suisse de 11 ans, doit comparaître aujourd'hui devant un tribunal du Colorado pour répondre de l'accusation d'inceste sur sa sœur de cinq ans.

Dénoncé en juin par une voisine qui affirme l'avoir vu enlever la culotte de sa petite sœur Sophia pour toucher ses organes génitaux, Raoul a été arrêté par la police dans la nuit du 30 août.

Les policiers l'ont réveillé, menotté, puis conduit dans une prison pour jeunes délinquants.

Raoul, 11, to appear before US justice for incest.

CHAPLEAU, *La Presse*, Montreal, November 9, 1999

NNA 1999 FINALIST

MACKINNON, *The Chronicle-Herald*, Halifax, January 10, 1999

TOM INNES (1923-2000)

ERIC BARDAL (1946-2000)

BEN WICKS (1926-2000)

DENNY PRITCHARD (1935-2000)

But, somehow, the Canadian version of the show simply failed to entertain local viewers.
WHO WANTS TO LOSE A BILLION EH?
Is it:
A. Human Resources?
B. NHL bailout?
C. Student loan risk premiums for banks?
D. Shawinigan pork?
Peterson
VANCOUVER SUN

Portfoolio 16

Thanks a Billion

Take my HRDC grants . . . please

Welcome, travellers. Welcome to *Portfoolio 16*, annual collection of the best editorial cartoons from across Canada. It's been a difficult voyage, we know: a year-long trip through the much anticipated chaos of the Y2K bug, infused with the excitement of reborn Joe Clarkmania, enlivened by the deeply engaging debate over the Clarity Bill and spiced by the nail-biting drama of the APEC inquiry, whose exciting conclusion provided one of the great twists in recent jurisprudence and which we will mock just as soon as we remember what it was.

But here at *Portfoolio*, where disrespecting our political masters is a 52-week-a-year job, we have decided that one story above all deserves the place of honour on our cover, representative for more than a decade and a half of the most egregious actions Canadian politics has to offer. And so we are pleased as punch to announce our co-winners: Jane Stewart and Jean Chrétien, co-authors of both the Human Resources porkbarrel and its subsequent explanation.

Of the former, it has become apparent that the distribution of a billion and a half dollars was to two places: hither and yon. Make that three places: hither, yon and Shawinigan. Of the latter, all we have to say is, things have come to a pretty pass when your position has to be explained by Jean Chrétien, the only Canadian ever to be declared a dangerous offender by the language police.

So come with us now to those thrilling days of yestermonth. The loan arranger rides again.

CLEMENT, *The National Post*

CORRIGAN, *The Toronto Star*

MACKINNON, *The Chronicle-Herald*, Halifax

—Me Tarzan, you Jane!

GARNOTTE, *Le Devoir*, Montreal

SAVING MINISTER STEWART

DOLIGHAN

MAYES, *The Edmonton Journal*

MAYES, *The Edmonton Journal*

DONATO, *The Toronto Sun*

MURPHY, *The Province*, Vancouver

GABLE, *The Globe & Mail*

HARROP, Back Bench

GABLE, *The Globe & Mail*

NEASE, *The Oakville Beaver*

MOU, *The Halifax Daily News*

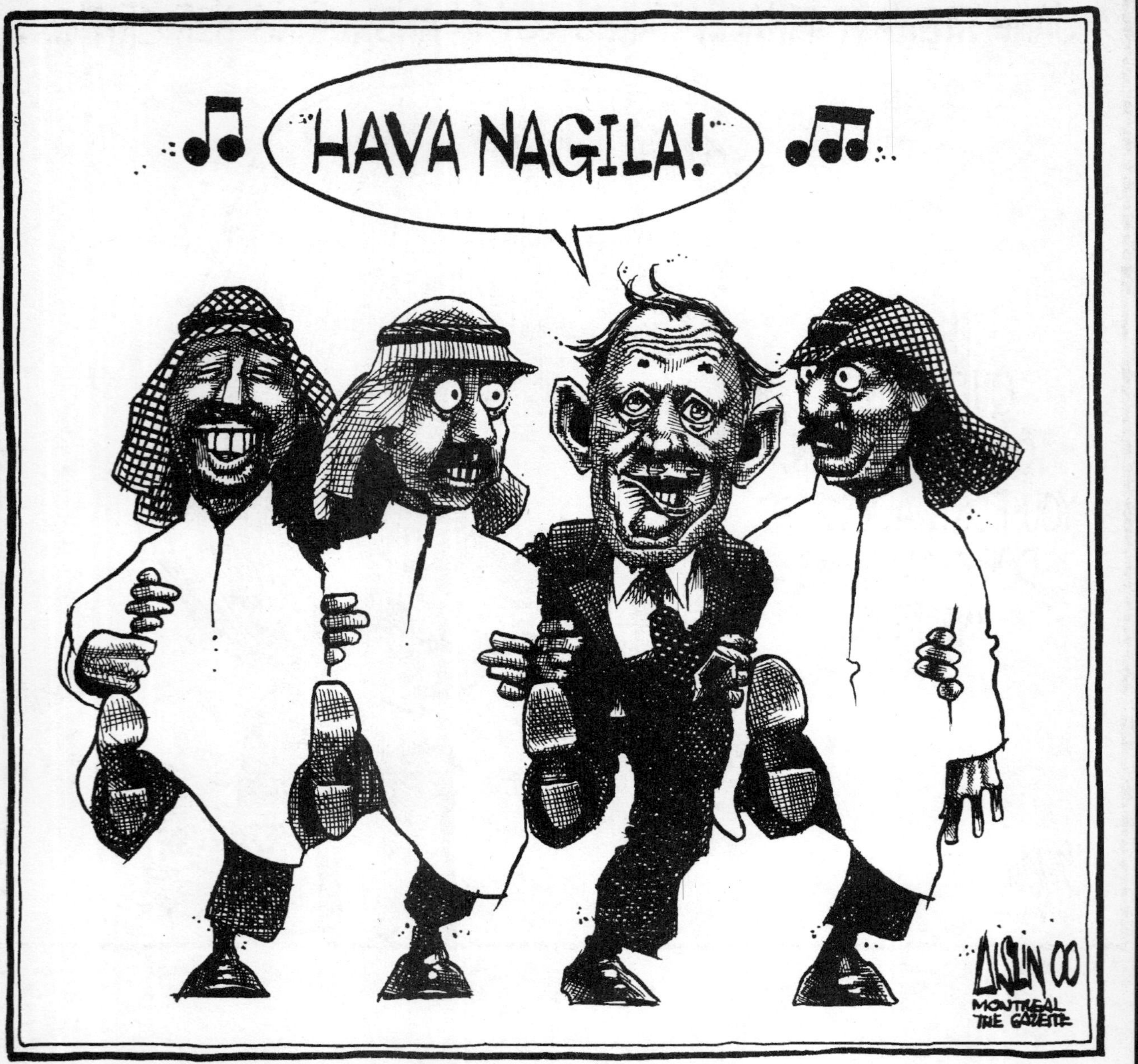
HAVA NAGILA!
AISLIN 00
MONTREAL THE GAZETTE

Portfoolio 16

Is This the Totality of Your Intelligence?

If this is Tuesday, this must be that place where all the Jewish people live

Canadian prime ministers have a sterling record of embarrassing everyone while they are in the Middle East (our theory: the mandatory yarmulke blocks the energy to the solar-powered prime ministerial brains) and Jean Chrétien's trip to the Holy Land more than lived down to our expectations. His off-the-cuff speech in Israel supporting the Palestinian right to a unilateral declaration of independence — a notion that rings vague bells just east of Ottawa — was the highlight of a trip in which he did everything but invite the Chief Rabbi out for bacon and eggs ("glass of milk with dat?").

His statesmanship brought support from all and sundry, notably Paul Martin, who abandoned his leadership hopes when he realized there could be worse things than being Finance Minister. An opening in Human Resources, for instance.

On wall: Cairo Museum, porcelain room (Do not touch)
—Faster! The Canadian is coming!

GARNOTTE, *Le Devoir*, Montreal

—That was quite a day!

CÔTÉ, *Le Soleil*, Quebec

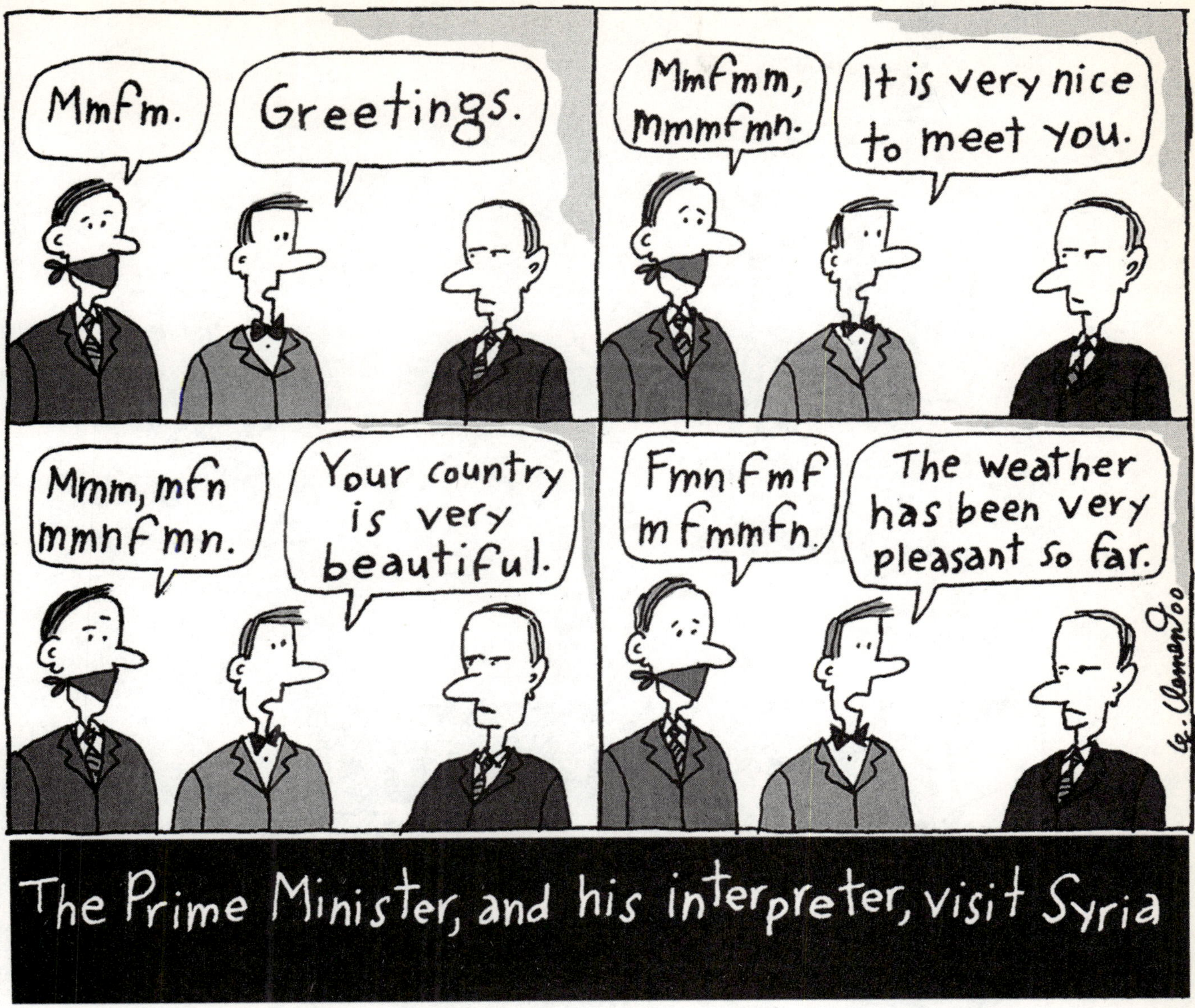

CLEMENT, *The National Post*

SPEAKING OF UNILATERAL DECLARATIONS OF INDEPENDENCE

LACHINE, *The Chatham Daily News*

NEASE, *The Oakville Beaver*

MACKINNON, *The Chronicle-Herald*, Halifax

ER... PAUL'S JUST STEPPED OUT FOR COFFEE.

JENKINS, *The Globe & Mail*

— Stop worring about Martin. Just because he's younger, has more hair and is better on T.V.

WICKS

MAYES, *The Edmonton Journal*

ME, Between Polls, *The Globe and Mail*

PAUL MARTIN'S RESPONSE TO LESSER DONS ACROSS CANADA DEMANDING MORE TRANSFER PAYMENTS...
Fuhgeddaboudit!
AISLIN 00
MONTREAL GAZETTE
The Liberos

Portfoolio 16

Aside From That, What Kind of Year Was It?

The elephant, the trough, the snail and other old favourites

Readers astute enough to have purchased this excellent volume will not need to be reminded that there was a budget this year (the elephant-sized surplus), the APEC inquiry did something (Chrétien and pepper spray), Alliance members decided to take government pensions after all (pigs at the trough) and the Hepatitis C decision was painfully slow (the snail).

These are the cartoonists' shorthand, the symbols by which we forever visualize the misbehaviour of public figures, just as we will later mourn their passing with the Statue of Liberty crying or flags being rent by bullet holes. We are happy to note that two new symbols have been added this year: Adrienne Clarkson, the new governor-general, and John Raulston Saul, her consort, have become regal throne-sitters, an image that will now haunt them yea unto retirement; and the members of Canada's CSIS spy agency — one of whom left top-secret documents in her car, whence they were stolen — have become putty-nosed clowns.

As have we all.

DUSAN, *The Toronto Star*

GABLE, *The Globe & Mail*

CORRIGAN, *The Toronto Star*

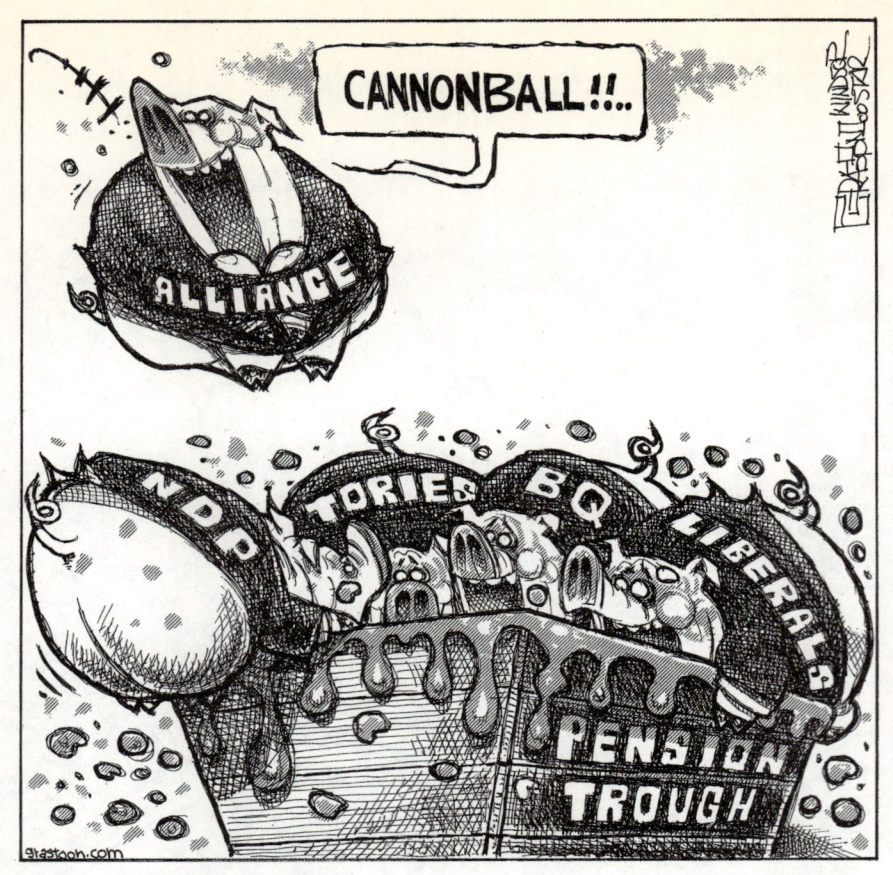

GRASTON, *The Windsor Star*

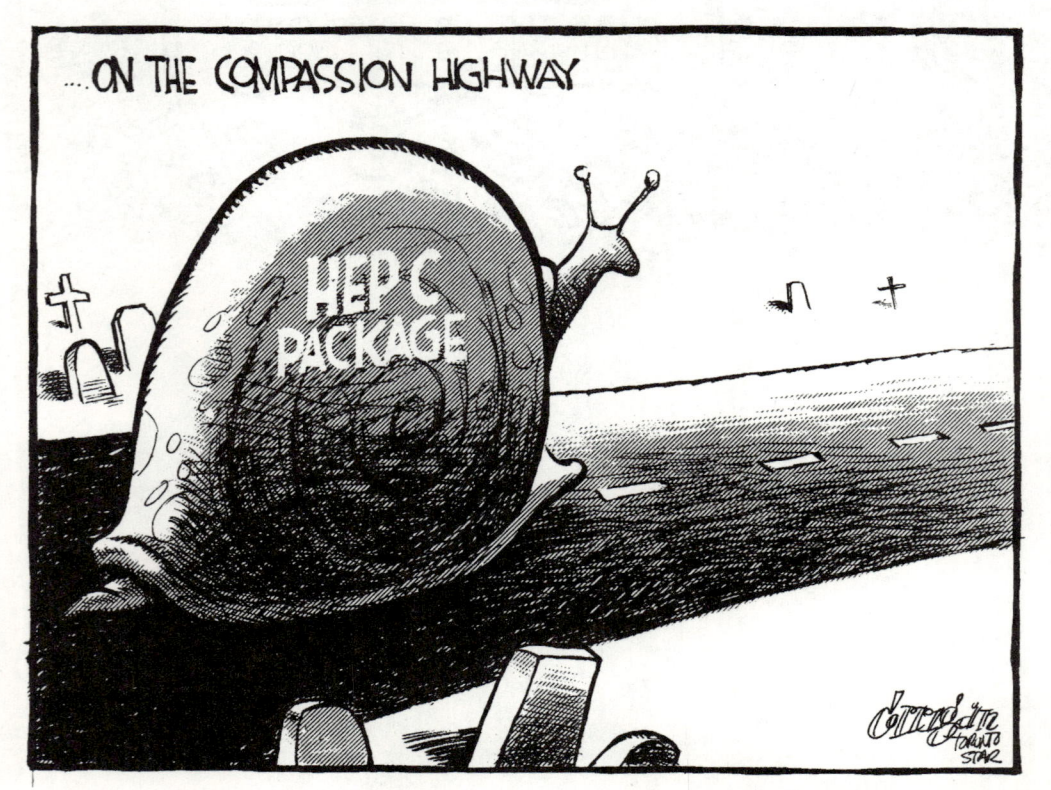

CORRIGAN, *The Toronto Star*

AISLIN, *The Gazette*, Montreal

Maternity Ward

LACHINE, *The Chatham Daily News*

"HE'S TOO DRUNK TO LIGHT THE CIGARETTE."

BIGGEST PROBLEM WITH USING RATS TO PROBE LINK BETWEEN BOOZE AND CIGARETTES.

HARROP, Back Bench

NEASE, *The Oakville Beaver*

Canadian focus groups disagree on icons for new currency design.

...just a suggestion.

PETERSON, *The Vancouver Sun*

ROSEN, *Hour*, Montreal

HARROP, *The Vancouver Sun*

CUMMINGS, *The Winnipeg Free Press*

LEFCOURT, *NOW*

.35

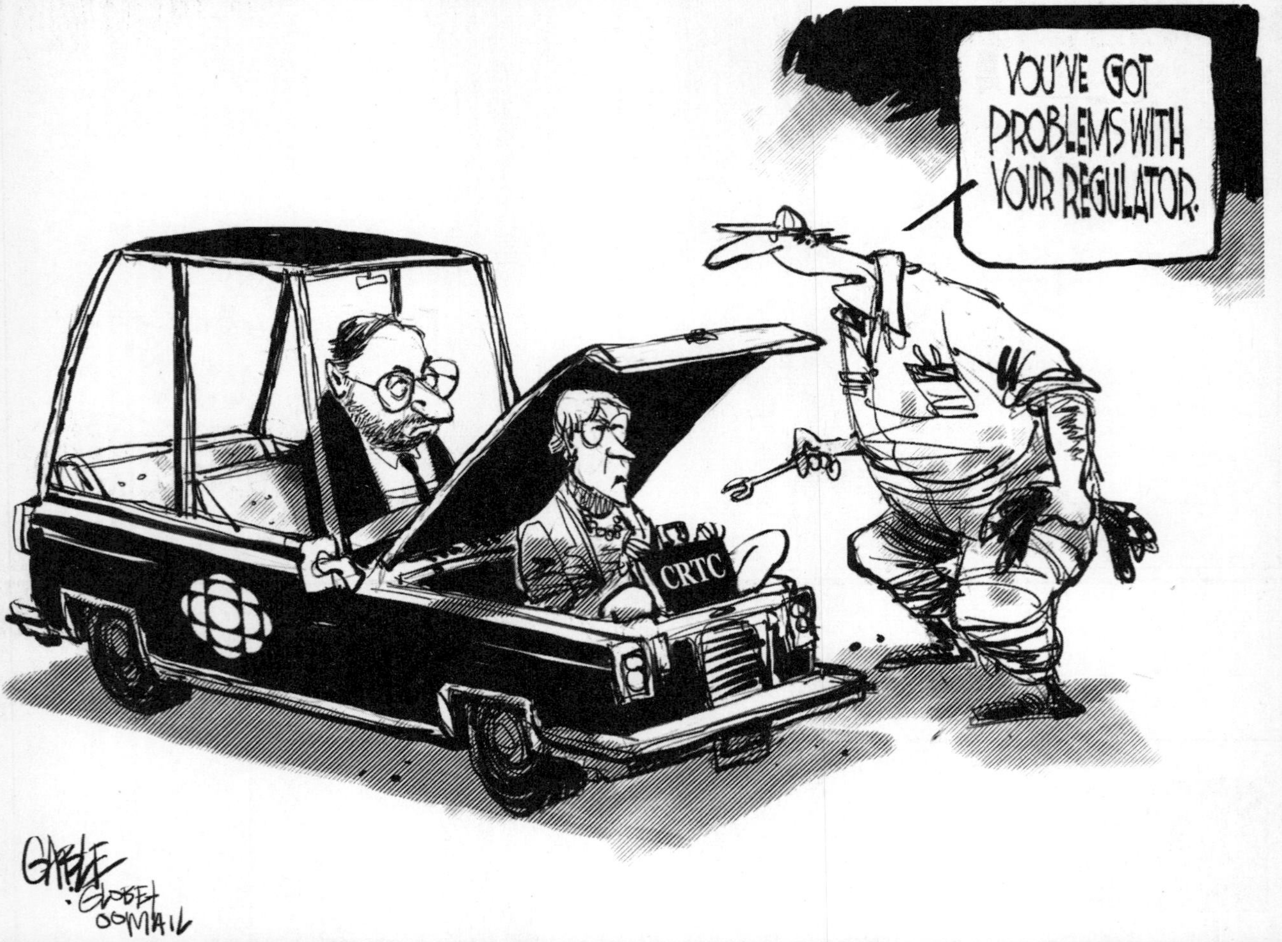
YOU'VE GOT PROBLEMS WITH YOUR REGULATOR.
CRTC

Portfoolio 16

Clearing the Air

You don't have to be Canadian to understand this section, but it helps

Two hardy perennials of the Canadian Experience have been entwined together for decades in the public mind: the Quebec referendum and the CBC. What usually happens is, the Quebec referendum is mentioned and you turn off the CBC. This year, however, the Corp became a story of its own, when its ever-deeper budget cuts threatened to turn it into a broadcast service dependent on several million empty tin cans and a thousand kilometres of string. The next step is apparently having Peter Mansbridge go door-to-door with updates.

As for Quebec, the Clarity Bill — a demand that Quebec have a clear question on its next referendum — caused a controversy that only a native Canadian, hardened by years in the language trenches, could understand. Outsiders might think clarity sounds like such a good idea it doesn't need its own bill, but we know the deeper truth: no matter what you propose, it will only remind everyone how unhappy they are. It simply raises that age-old conundrum: Obscurity, a Federal or Provincial Responsibility?

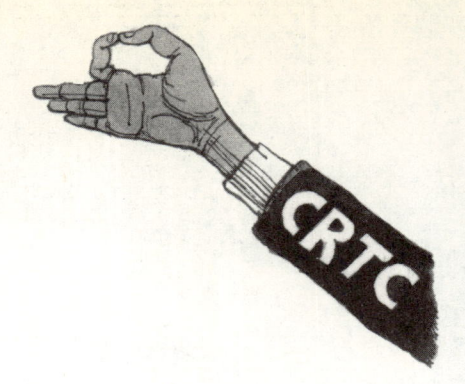

DUSAN, *The Toronto Star*

ME, Between Polls, *The Globe and Mail*

CUMMINGS, *The Winnipeg Free Press*

DE ADDER, *The Chronicle-Herald*, Halifax

— That ... is not a clear majority!

CÔTÉ, *Le Soleil*, Quebec

AISLIN, *The Gazette*, Montreal

MAYES, *The Edmonton Journal*

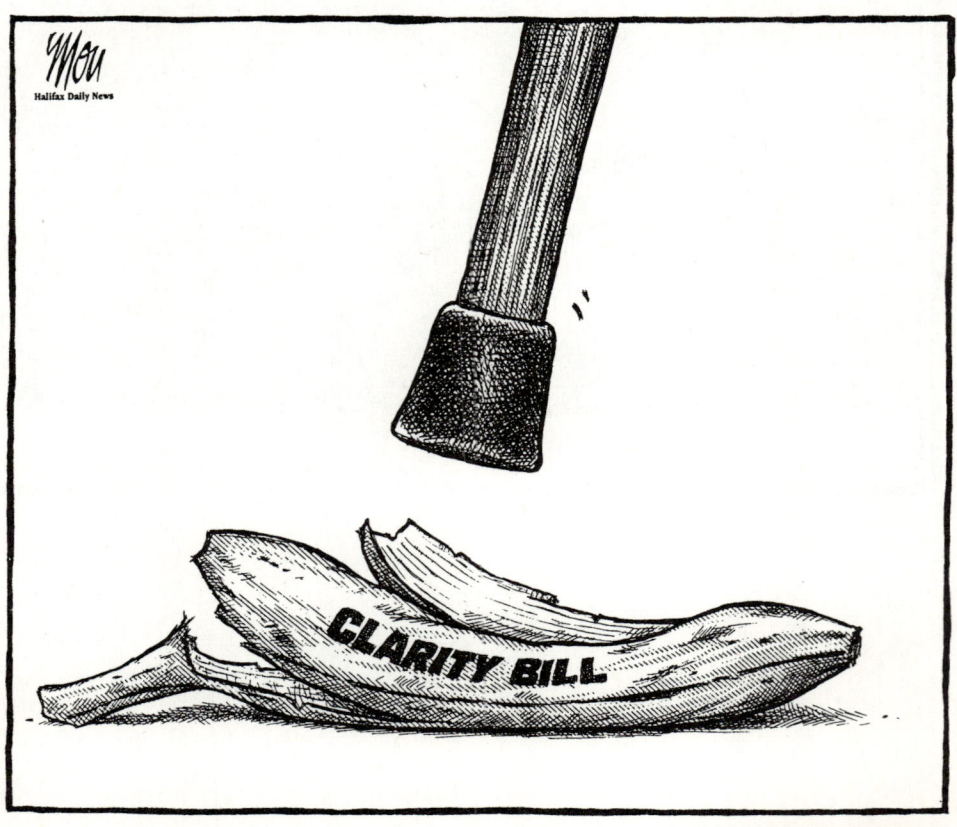

MOU, *The Halifax Daily News*

MACKAY, *The Hamilton Spectator*

LACHINE, *The Chatham Daily News*

In order to speed up the vote on clarity, MPs won't have to stand up...
— ...They can remain on their knees!

GODIN

AISLIN, *The Gazette*, Montreal

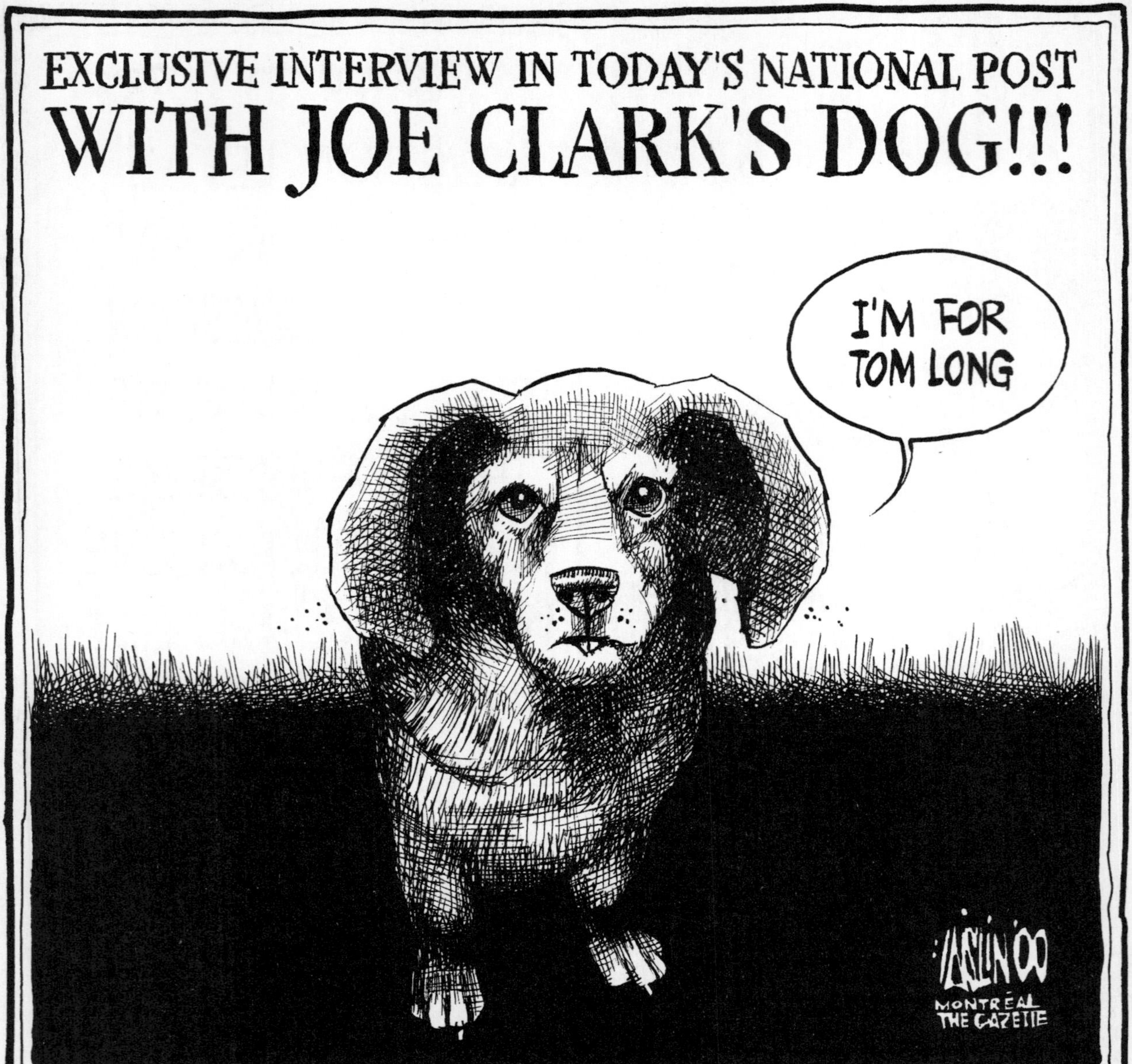
EXCLUSIVE INTERVIEW IN TODAY'S NATIONAL POST
WITH JOE CLARK'S DOG!!!
I'M FOR TOM LONG
AISLIN '00
MONTRÉAL THE GAZETTE

Portfoolio 16

My Name Is Joe
In which the Alliance and the Conservatives stand cheek by jowl

Canada got a new political party this year, which was for a while called CCRAP, such a thuddingly obvious target that our more delicate satirists seriously pondered letting it go by: what glory in hitting doubles off the wall if they're serving up batting-practice pitches? Stockwell Day, whose name sounds like a one-time-only sale at a failing department store, is a new, fun-to-draw face on the political scene, but he'll have a ways to go to match Joe Clark, the hall-of-fame caricature who appears not to have been born as much as ordered from room service by the cartoonists' union. Joe, each day looking more like a boiled potato with wattles, suffered through several party defections. He was passionately irrelevant. It was as if John Diefenbaker had been reborn in the middle of a rap concert. Joe is regarded with affection by our artists; he is a living link to the past we never had.

MAYES, *The Edmonton Journal*

HARROP, Back Bench

CUMMINGS, *The Winnipeg Free Press*

CLEMENT, The National Post

NEASE, *The Oakville Beaver*

WICKS, *The Outcasts*

Cartoon 1 — "SELLING 'MR. RIGHT'"

- Born in Ontario!
- Not Preston Manning
- Ontario born!
- Not Joe Clark
- Knows all the words to 'Ontari~ari~ario'
- Definitely born in Ontario!
- Yes, born in Ontario!
- Not Brian Mulroney
- His name alone inspires the TSE
- Not John Diefenbaker
- Has lived in Ottawa!
- And did we mention ...born in Ontario?

(Briefcase: STOCKWELL DAY — CANADIAN ALLIANCE WOTZIT)

PETERSON, *The Vancouver Sun*

Cartoon 2

"ay Pride"

"Day Pride" / "Alliance"

INCREASINGLY DARYL BEGAN TO SUSPECT HE WAS AT THE WRONG RALLY...

GABLE, *The Globe & Mail*

Just Another Day on the Job...

Preston Manning

SEBASTIAN

GABLE, *The Globe & Mail*

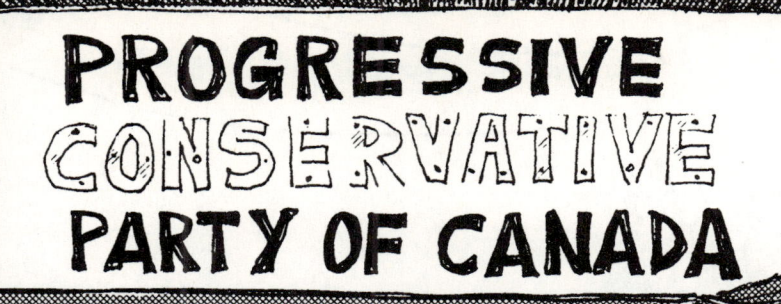

LARTER, The Calgary Sun

JENKINS, *The Globe & Mail*

GARNOTTE, *Le Devoir*, Montreal

"The Alliance is nothing but a bunch of **MEAN-SPIRITED, SLACK-JAWED TROGLODYTES!**
...any of whom are welcome back to the fold."

SEBASTIAN

LACHINE, *The Chatham Daily News*

— Okay, okay. Mr. Clark. Yes I'm still with you, cross my heart. Now can I go back to bed.

WICKS

GABLE, *The Globe & Mail*

DE ADDER, Cabinet Shuffles

ROSEN, Hour, Montreal

MACKAY, *The Hamilton Spectator*

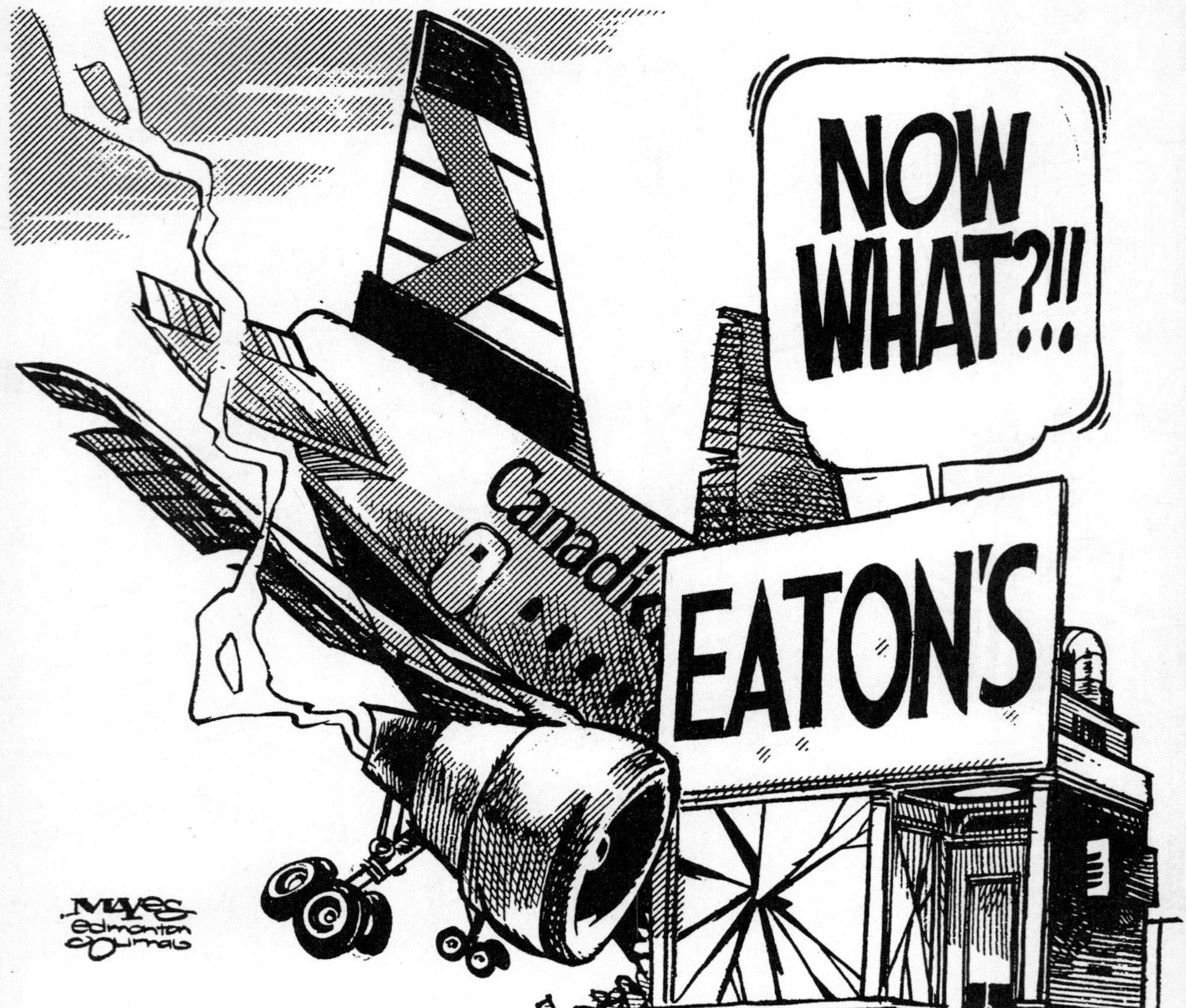
NOW WHAT?!...
Canadi
EATON'S
MAYES
edmonton journal

Portfoolio 16

Fuel Prices Up, Health Care Down

Or, as the sign on the highway said, Eat Here and Get Gas

Bad things happened to Canadian institutions this year: the last spike for 1,900 CP Rail jobs, the last straw for Eaton's. It was a sad end for a store that wasn't so much a part of our history as a part of our myth. "Satisfaction guaranteed or money refunded," they said, and an entire nation turned up at the returns counter.

Canadian Airlines was also heading toward oblivion under the new ownership of Air Canada, which merged the airline, forwarded it to Hong Kong by mistake, but is even now putting out a tracer. It should reappear any day.

Health care, meanwhile, once the source of great Canadian pride, was gradually devolving into the much feared two-tier system or, in some cases, the many-tear system. We would have driven to the United States for that check-up, but the gas prices went so high you needed an HRDC grant to fill up.

In the midst of all this, more jobs were being cut, mostly by the banks, which have now been so depopulated that robbers have to send in their hold-up notes on the Internet. And our old friend the fat hog makes a guest appearance in this section, unless Jean Chrétien has already appointed him ambassador to Israel.

— THE LAST SPIKE —

CRAIG, *The Western Producer*

EATON

ROSEN, *Hour*, Montreal

CUMMINGS, *The Winnipeg Free Press*

ME, Between Polls, *The Globe and Mail*

DUSAN, *The Toronto Star*

— What time is the next fare increase?

WICKS

CLEMENT, *The National Post*

"THINGS ARE LOOKING UP, LOIS YOU'RE NEXT IN LINE FOR RADIATION THERAPY"

"YOU KNOW THAT HEART SURGERY YOU WERE WAITING FOR?.."

"GOOD NEWS, PHIL. A HOSPITAL BED JUST OPENED UP"

MORE EVIDENCE OF A HEALTH CARE SYSTEM IN CRISIS

RICE

"IF THE PROVINCES WANT TO ENSURE MORE MONEY FOR HEALTH"

"THEY SHOULD MOVE THEIR HOSPITALS TO SHAWINIGAN."

MOU, *The Halifax Daily News*

TWO-TIER HEALTH CARE

BADO, *Le Droit*, Ottawa

MAYES, *The Edmonton Journal*

WICKS

GRASTON, *The Windsor Star*

FEWINGS

CORRIGAN, *The Toronto Star*

DUSAN, *The Toronto Star*

AISLIN, *The Gazette*, Montreal

DOLIGHAN

GRASTON, *The Windsor Star*

BRAIN DRAIN

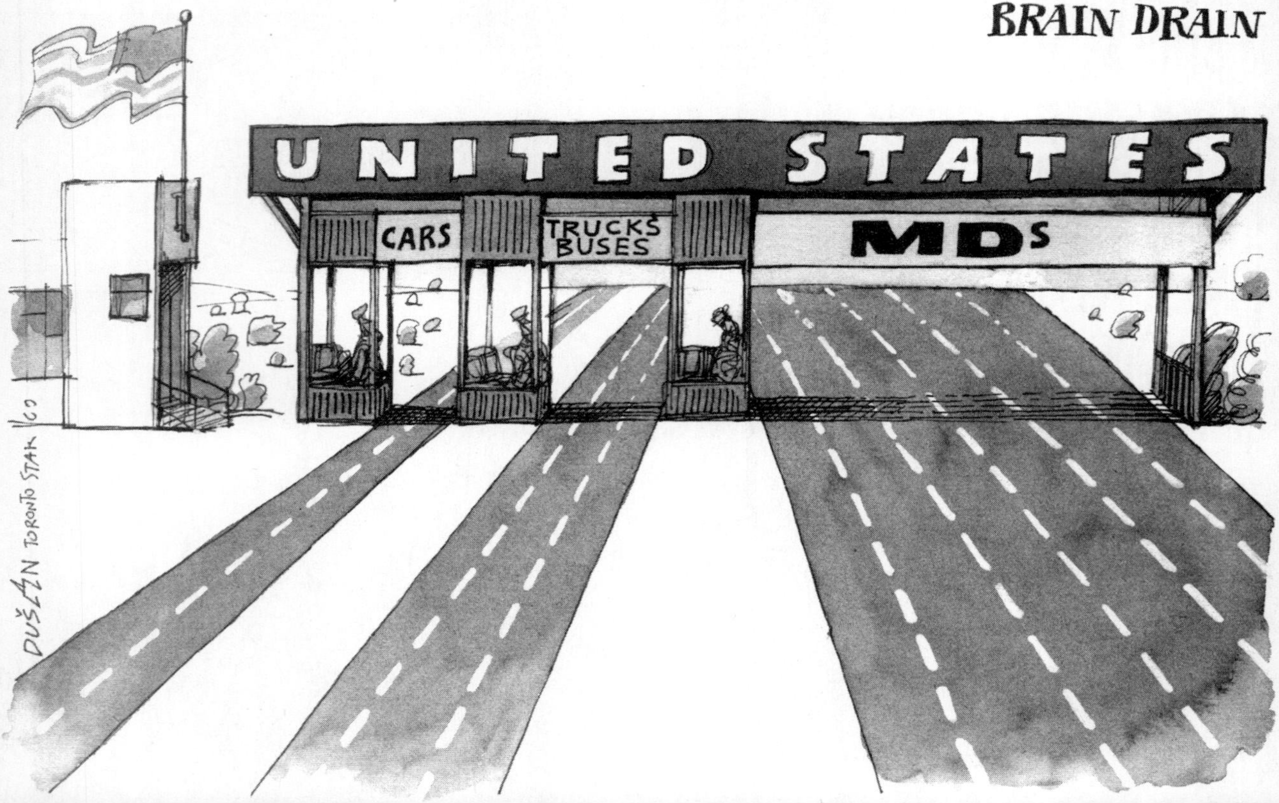

Portfoolio 16

The Best and the Rightest

Will the last brain to leave the country please close the drain?

Doctors, computer experts and other worthies were alleged to be leaving Canada in record numbers, to be replaced by boatloads of hungry-eyed Asians who crowded aboard leaky freighters in a desperate rush to our shores. So far, the confirmed numbers have 10 professionals out of the country and 150 illegal immigrants in, but the trend is there all the same.

Among those going is Conrad Black, who had his own problems with Jean Chrétien when he was denied permission to become a British lord. It has always been our position that anyone who wants to be in the House of Lords deserves to be put there, and speaking as an employee of one of Conrad Black's newspapers, I mean that in the nicest possible way, sir.

As for the NHL, not only players but entire teams were threatening to flee to the United States to take advantage of the more benevolent tax system, not to mention the superior health care they will need. Head injuries are on the rise, which (funnily enough) brings us back to the brain drain.

RICE

DUSAN, *The Toronto Star*

MAYES, *The Edmonton Journal*

ME, Between Polls, *The Globe and Mail*

AISLIN, *The Gazette*, Montreal

J, *The Globe & Mail*

PETERSON, *The Vancouver Sun*

—They visit us sometimes!

BADO, *Le Droit*, Ottawa

HARROP, Back Bench

CUMMINGS, *The Winnipeg Free Press*

MACKINNON, *The Chronicle-Herald*, Halifax

WELCOME TO
ONTARIO
HOME OF THE 30% TAX-CUT
PLEASE DON'T DRINK THE WATER

Portfoolio 16

Don't Go Near the Water

In which the deficit-cutting chickens come home to roost in a stew of mixed-metaphor bad water

Things went along pretty much as usual across the land. B.C. kicked out its leaders, Alberta moved further to the right in what looked for all the world like some neo-con romantic instinct to nuzzle up to Ontario, if not mate with her, and Ontario was so busy setting new standards for its beleaguered teachers that it forgot about setting old standards for the stuff that comes out of its taps. The H was a little too O, as they say. Some blamed cuts in the Environment Ministry, others saw it as just another big toxic drip in the province. The two favourite exports of the Maritimes — lobster and Ashley MacIsaac — both became endangered. One couldn't fill the traps and the other couldn't shut his. The good news is, nothing really stupid happened in Manitoba. Or at least nothing you could draw.

"IT APPEARS MY FIRST TASK AS LEADER IS PRETTY CLEAR..."

DOLIGHAN
dolighant@aol.com

DOLIGHAN

"WHAT A GREAT SUNDECK! WHAT'S THE TRAPDOOR FOR?"

MAYES, *The Edmonton Journal*

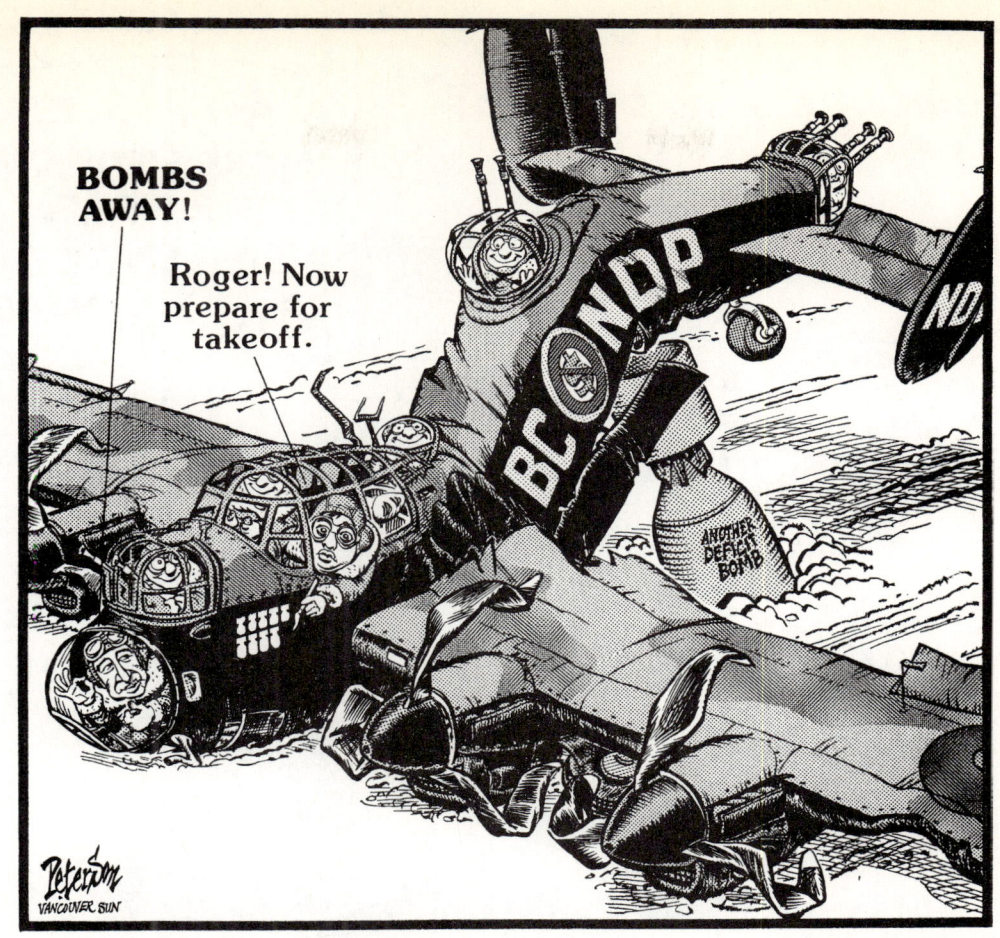

PETERSON, *The Vancouver Sun*

LEFCOURT

RICE

LIND, *Weltschmerz*

ANDY, *The National Post*

NEASE, *The Oakville Beaver*

.89

DUSAN, *The Toronto Star*

JÉ, *Hazardous Materials Management Magazine*

GABLE, *The Globe & Mail*

GRASTON, *The Windsor Star*

GABLE, *The Globe & Mail*

DUSAN, *The Toronto Star*

CORRIGAN, *The Toronto Star*

HOGAN

MOU, *The Halifax Daily News*

MURPHY, *The Province*, Vancouver

the first star....

Portfoolio 16

Un Canadien Errant

A farewell to Maurice Richard, but to little else

"The Rocket's Red Glare," they said of him, and "The First Star." Maurice Richard was remembered across Quebec, and Canada, as the hockey legend who scored 50 goals in 50 games when both of them meant something, who galvanized the province with his pride and the country with his intensity. Maurice Richard was a hero. He was not only a symbol for Quebec, he was the last such symbol some of us ever understood — the best player in a game where the winners and losers were easy to determine and clarity came in the speed of a wrist shot rather than from law-makers.

Speaking of which, Bill 101 was still in the news after all these years, helped along by chief language-watcher Louise Beaudoin, who declared that the French in France was not French enough, although it was certainly French enough if you didn't understand it, which is another advantage of unilingualism. Personally, we've been eating french fries and french toast all our life and we still don't get Jerry Lewis.

A Montreal company called Cinar got in trouble for crediting America-written TV scripts to Canadian writers so it would be eligible for federal grants. The scripts were fine otherwise, but they weren't Canadian enough, a welcome switch.

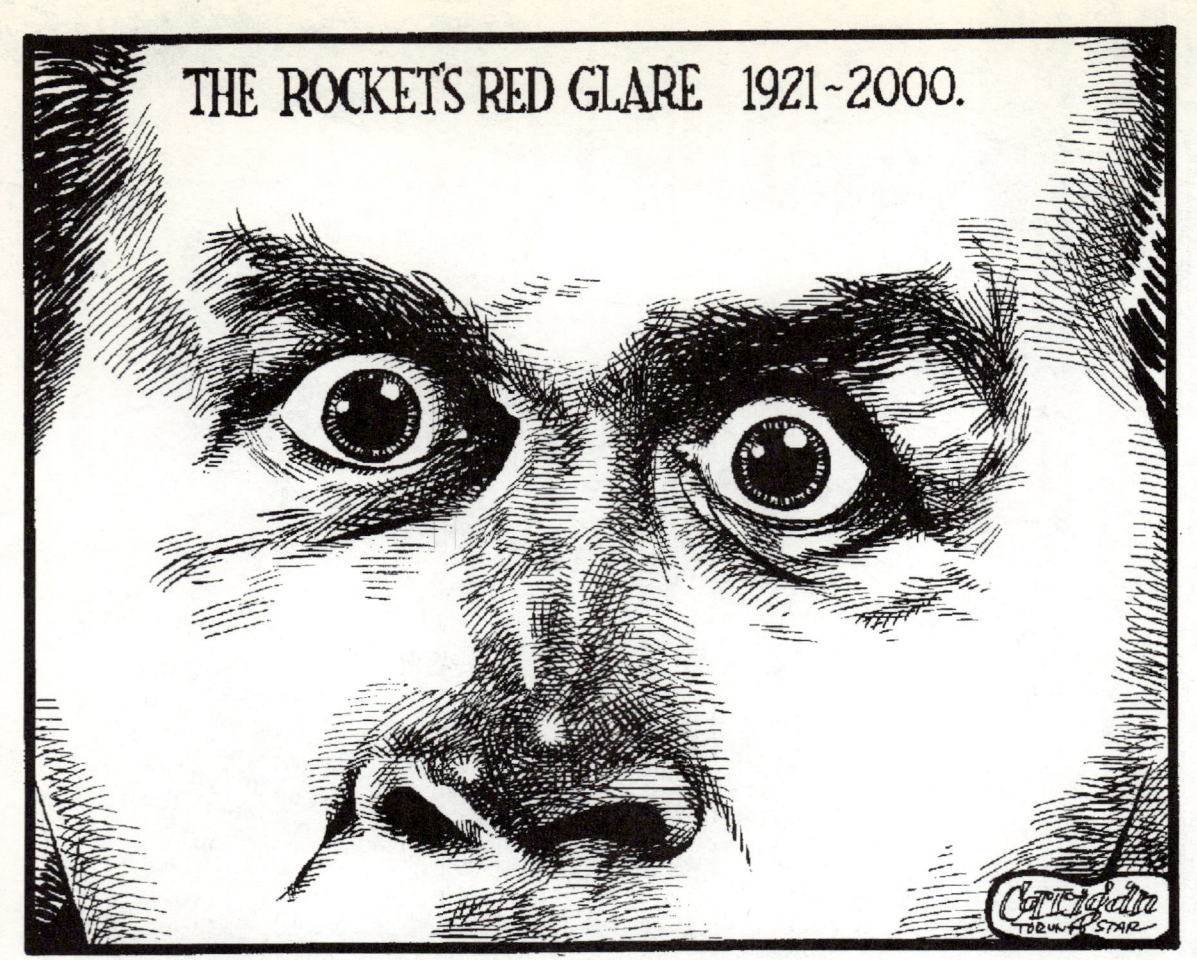

CORRIGAN, *The Toronto Star*

AISLIN, *The Gazette*, Montreal

GRASTON, *The Windsor Star*

CLEMENT, *The National Post*

HARROP, Back Bench

AISLIN, *The Gazette*, Montreal

The Further Adventures of Arthur...

> HEY! WHERE THE HELL'S MY WALLET?

ROSEN, *Hour*, Montreal

> ...ET L'OSCAR DU MEILLEUR PRÊTE-NOM CANADIEN POUR UN SCÉNARISTE AMÉRICAIN VA 'A...

UNITED STATES ACADEMY OF MOTION PICTURE

— ...and the Oscar for best Canadian alias for an American script writer goes to...

GARNOTTE, *Le Devoir*, Montreal

AISLIN, *The Gazette*, Montreal

WANTS TO MARRY A MULTI-ONAIRE
FOX
CANCELLED
AGGGGH!
AGGGGGH!!
WHO WA
TO
BE A
MILL
PLAN B...
grastoon.com

Portfoolio 16

Amber Waves of Pain

As they say in the NRA, Is That Your Final Answer?

He gave us some of the most memorable characters in the history of the comics: a beagle who dreamed of First World War glory, a self-possessed young girl who dreamed she ruled the world, a round-headed young boy who dreamed of anything at all. Charles Schulz made life's disappointments humorous, and he made its struggles touching, and the funny pages are a little less funny with his passing.

The same can't be said for the adults surrounding Elian Gonzalez, the young Cuban boy who washed up on American shores as a symbol of the struggle between communism and capitalism. Young boys usually don't do well as symbols, but Elian managed to fill the role: the perfect metaphor for the excesses of the American political/cultural/media circus so sorely missed since OJ was let off.

Welcome distraction came with a new television show that had everyone asking a now-famous catchphrase: how can these people be so stupid?

NEASE, *The Oakville Beaver*

DONATO, *The Toronto Sun*

CÔTÉ, *Le Soleil*, Quebec

BADO, *Le Droit*, Ottawa

CLEMENT, *The National Post*

ANDY, Cartoonists & Writers Syndicate

MACKAY, *The Hamilton Spectator*

LARTER, *The Calgary Sun*

ELIAN GONZALEZ
ADRIFT AT SEA

DITTO   DITTO

GABLE, *The Globe & Mail*

EN RESTANT ICI, ON T'ÉVITE
D'ÊTRE PRISONNIER À CUBA!

—By remaining here, you avoid being a prisoner in Cuba!

BADO, *Le Droit*, Ottawa

LE «PETIT» ELIAN...

"Little Elian"...

GARNOTTE, *Le Devoir*, Montreal

—Is it true that I'll be brainwashed in Cuba?

CÔTÉ, *Le Soleil*, Quebec

SEBASTIAN

WHY JANET RENO SHOULD NEVER HAVE CHILDREN.

"DIDN'T I TELL YOU TO CLEAN UP YOUR ROOM?"

RICE

NEASE, *The Oakville Beaver*

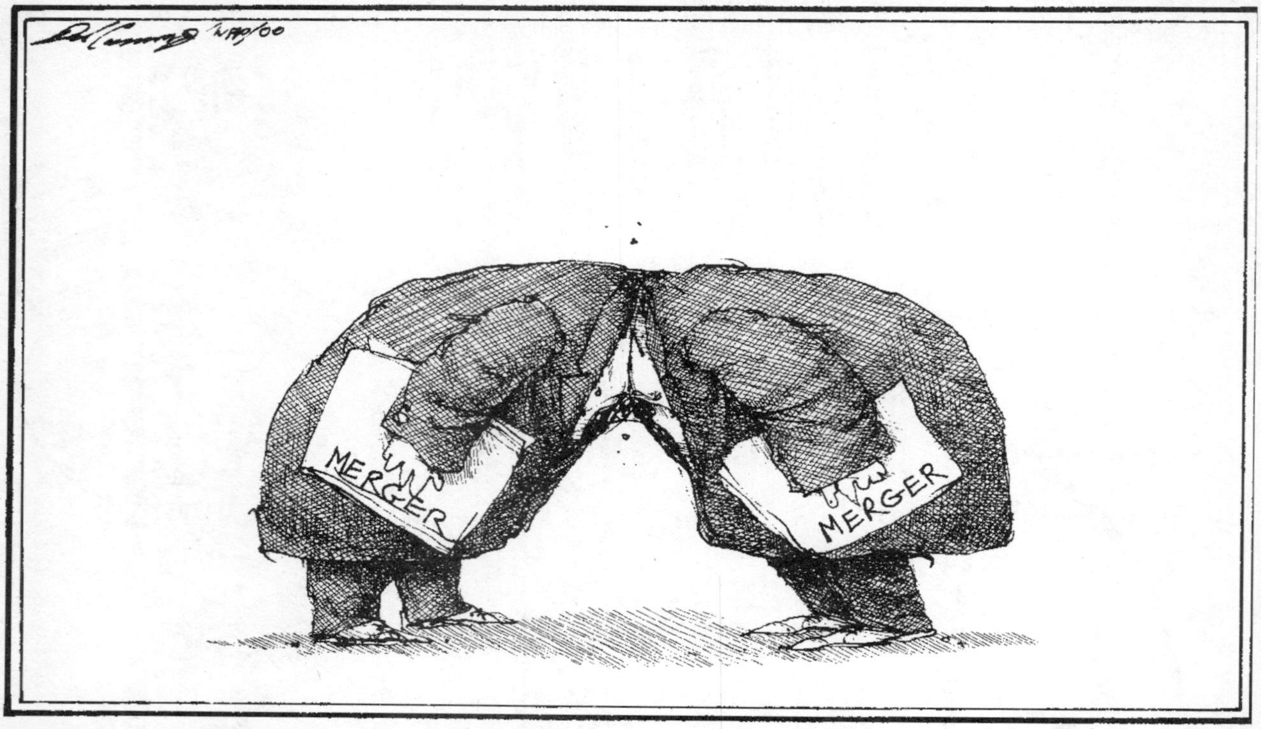
MERGER
MERGER

Portfoolio 16

Open Up Those Golden Gates

A potpourri of mergers, shootings, political scandals and other American sports

In economic news from our southern neighbour, large corporations merged and larger ones were told to unmerge, which provided useful employment for federal regulators. Americans continued to exercise their constitutional right to bear arms, often on school grounds. This was defended by the National Rifle Association and its new leader, Charlton Heston, one of a series of Hollywood actors who derive their political clout from their screen images — in Heston's case a famous scene in which God provides the Second Amendment to the 10 Commandments. It makes you wonder what would have happened if Warren Beatty had followed through on his threat to join the U.S. presidential race. He didn't, and America was spared the sight of a famous womanizer bringing an unwelcome aura of sexuality to the White House.

Following financial setbacks, Bill Gates turns to busking

MURPHY, *The Province*, Vancouver

LEFT TO HIS OWN DEVICES BILL GATES COMES UP WITH A WAY TO SPLIT MICROSOFT:

MEET MINI BILL

RICE

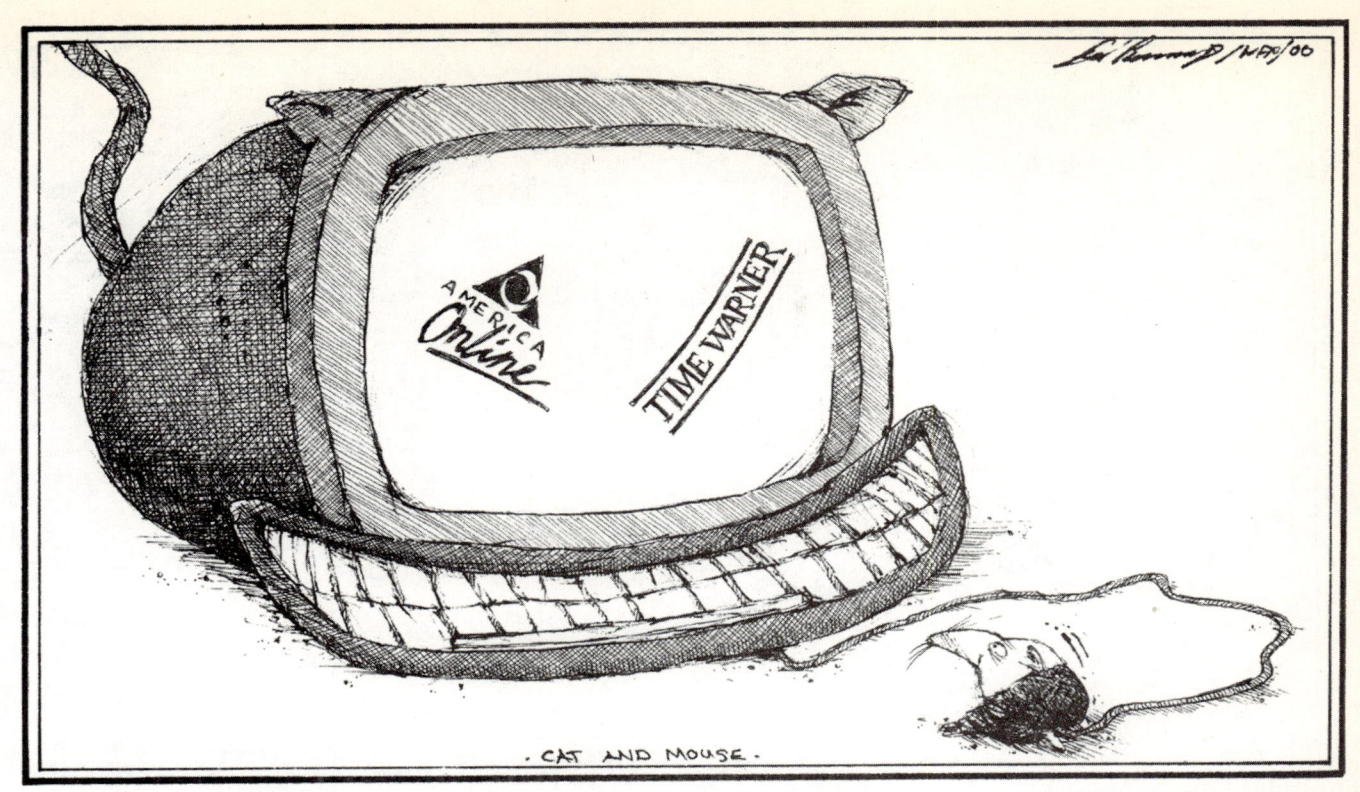

CUMMINGS, *The Winnipeg Free Press*

"Looks as if there might really be something to those take-over rumors."

JÉ, *The National Post*

CUMMINGS, *The Winnipeg Free Press*

School American style...
—Thanks for the chalk!

GARNOTTE, *Le Devoir*, Montreal

DUSAN, *The Toronto Star*

LEA

Charlton Heston re-elected president of National Rifle Association

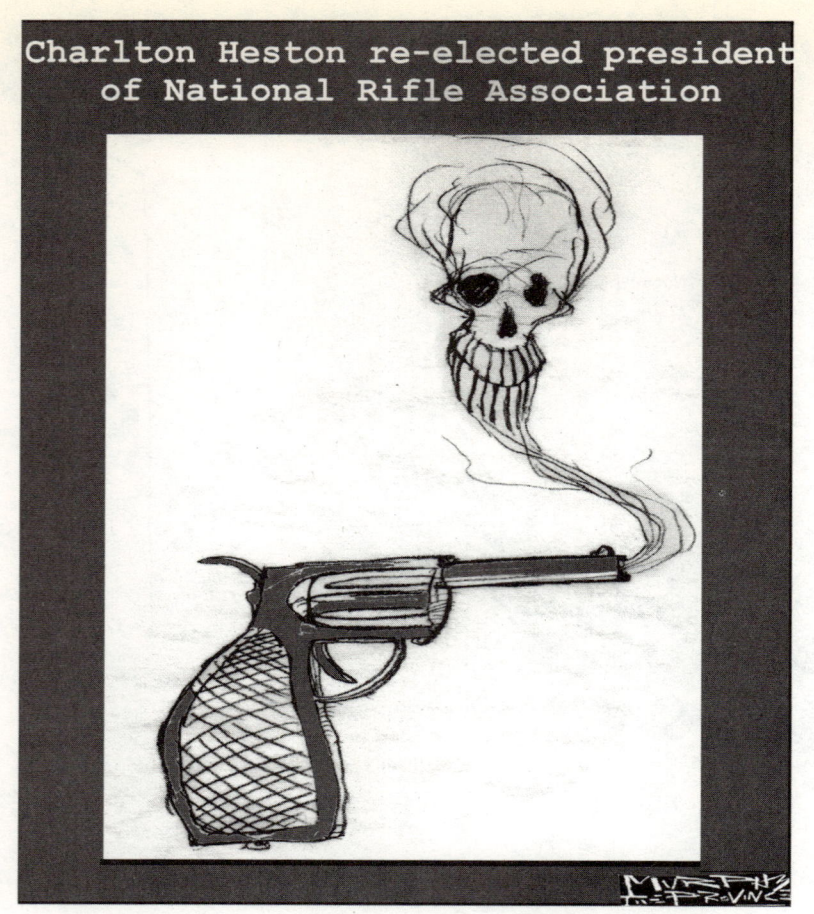

MURPHY, *The Province*, Vancouver

IF YOU CAN GET YOUR FORMER GIRLFRIENDS TO VOTE FOR YOU, WE CAN TAKE THE ENTIRE MIDWEST...

BEATTY FOR PRESIDENT

HARROP

Geo. W. BUSH

whiff of scandal

MURPHY, Artizans

GARNOTTE, *Le Devoir*, Montreal

FATHER, WITHOUT GOING INTO TOO MANY DETAILS, I ASK FORGIVENESS FOR SINS COMMITED BY MANY OF OUR PEOPLE, GOING BACK A NUMBER OF YEARS.
HIS HOLINESS?
NO, HELMUT KOHL.
ANDY '00

Portfoolio 16

Rights and Wrongs

The fascist ghosts of the old days meet the violent realities of the new

The world's trouble spots were so numerous this year we can provide only a sampler of the devastation, most of it aimed at innocent civilians in Grozny, East Timor, and Northern Ireland. Worst, perhaps, was Sierra Leone, one of many African nations where brutal armies chopped and hacked their way through human decency. If there is an image of inhumanity for the 21st century, it is of the Africans who have been disfigured and abandoned, left armless, legless, and most wrenching of all, without hope.

World leaders who made the news were mostly connected to brutalities of years gone by. The Pope apologized for the Vatican's failure to help the Jews during the Nazi years; Austria's Joerg Haider was elected and then quit when he was accused of wanting to bring back those years; Chile's General Pinochet, who did bring them back, was arrested and then released on the grounds of illness — moral enfeeblement, perhaps? It was almost a relief to see that Germany's Helmut Kohl was guilty of nothing more than taking bribes. In the world of 2000, this was a ray of sunshine.

RUSSIAN ROULETTE

GABLE, *The Globe & Mail*

SURPRISE!

BADO, *Le Droit*, Ottawa

CLEMENT, *The National Post*

CUMMINGS, *The Winnipeg Free Press*

RÉPONSE TIMORÉE

Timorous response.   BADO, *Le Droit*, Ottawa

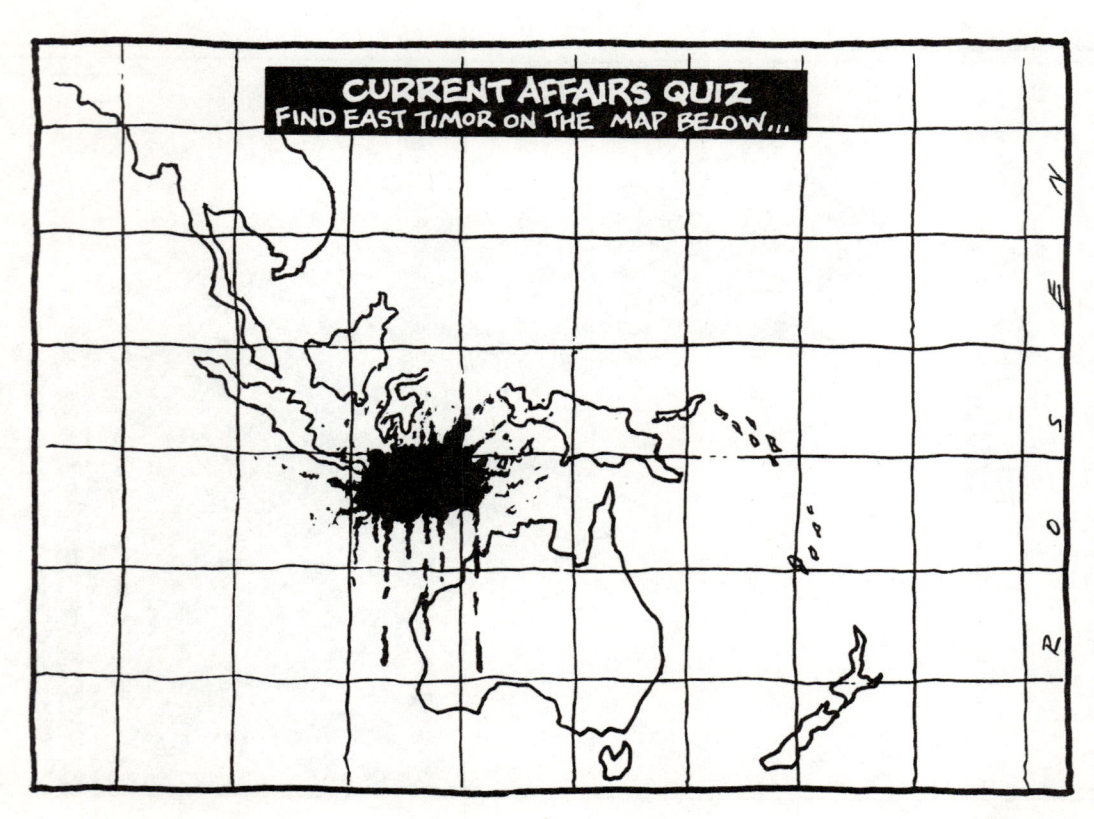

ROSEN, *Hour*, Montreal

CORRIGAN, *The Toronto Star*

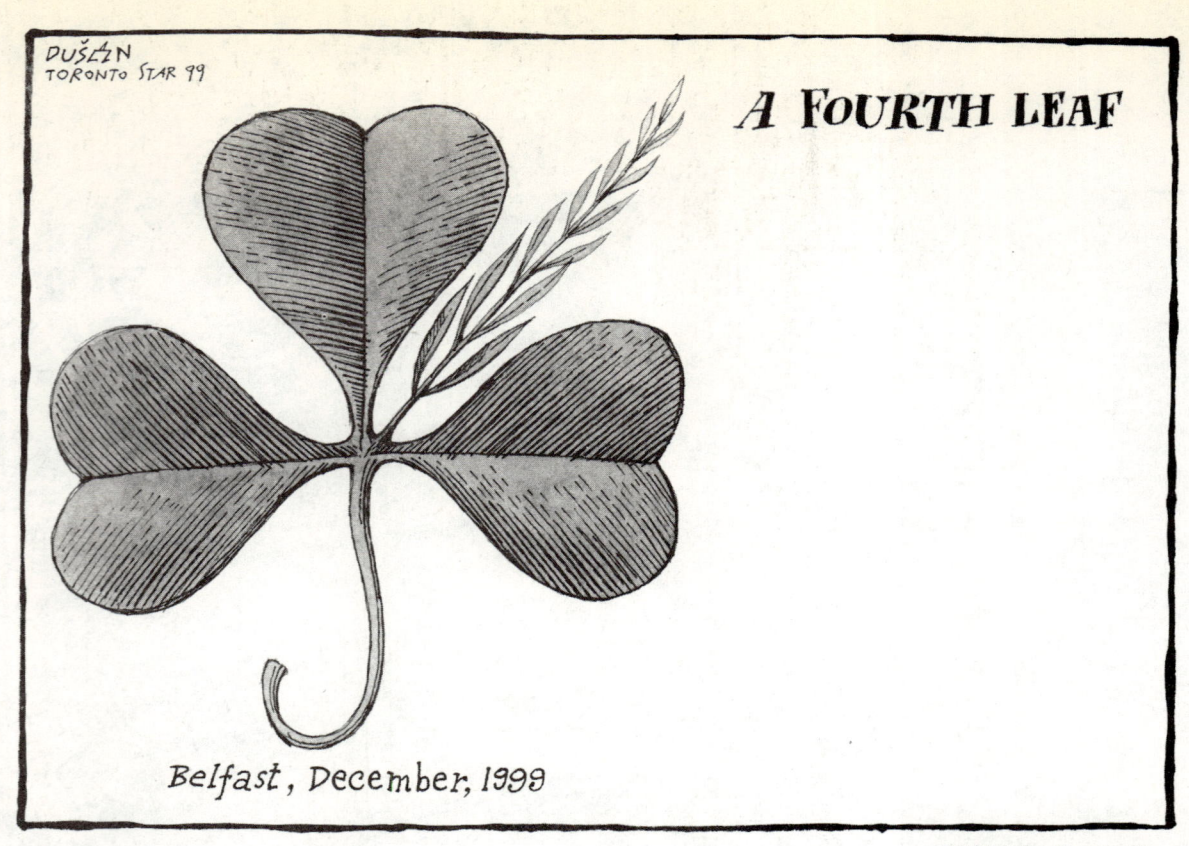

A Fourth Leaf

Belfast, December, 1999

DUSAN, *The Toronto Star*

MACKINNON, *The Chronicle-Herald*, Halifax

PETERSON, *The Vancouver Sun*

DE ADDER, *The Chronicle-Herald*, Halifax

GABLE, *The Globe & Mail*

CUMMINGS, *The Winnipeg Free Press*

DOLIGHAN

CLEMENT, *The National Post*

MURPHY, Artizans

RIGHT! RIGHT! RIGHT, RIGHT, RIGHT!

DANSE MACABRE

PETERSON, *The Vancouver Sun*

"TOO INFIRM TO STAND TRIAL"

TOO DEAD TO STAND UP

CORRIGAN, *The Toronto Star*

AISLIN, *The Gazette*, Montreal

—It's the little things you miss!   GARNOTTE, *Le Devoir*, Montreal

—I don't feel too well myself!   BADO, *Le Droit*, Ottawa

Pinochet

SEBASTIAN

How the heck did they figure it came from the Philippines?
ILOVEYOU
ILOVEYOU
ILOVEYOU
ILOVEYOU
Manila envelopes.
ILOVEYOU
ILOVEYOU
ILOVEYOU
ILOVEYOU

Portfoolio 16

I Love You
Warning: Open This Section at Your Peril

This was the year of the computer virus, a kind of electronic vandalism that is the high-tech version of ordering pizza for your neighbours and then watching the fun through the living room drapes. In this case, the neighbours lived 3,000 kilometres away and the pizza was a note entitled I Love You that could wipe out their hard drives, but the instinct for mindless pranks was the same.

People were also talking about genetically altered foods, a scientific program by which fruits and vegetables are made bigger and better through a little tweaking of their DNA, with absolutely no chance that consumers would later grow two heads or glow in the dark. Many who thought this would lead to cases of Mad Radish Disease also gathered in Seattle to protest the World Trade Organization. Their philosophical errors were explained at the point of a billy club.

The good news was that the chaos of the much-feared millennium bug did not occur. For those who prefer their chaos to be organic, this was a cheery development indeed.

CLEMENT, *The National Post*

"I'm sorry sir, but I don't think we stock genetically modified foods."

JÉ, *The Ottawa Citizen*

GABLE, The Globe & Mail

GLOBALIZATION

DUSAN, *The Toronto Star*

THE GAP

DUSAN, *The Toronto Star*

CLEMENT, *The National Post*

ANDY, Cartoonists & Writers Syndicate

BIOGRAPHIES

AISLIN is the name of TERRY MOSHER's elder daughter and the *nom de plume* he uses as the editorial page cartoonist for the Montreal *Gazette*. Syndicated throughout Canada, he has freelanced in the U.S. and abroad for *The New York Times*, *Time*, *The National Lampoon*, *Harper's*, *The Atlantic Monthly* and *Punch*.

Mosher was born in Ottawa in 1942 and attended fourteen different schools in Montreal, Toronto and Quebec City, graduating from the Ecole des Beaux-arts in 1967. He then began working for *The Montreal Star*, moving over to *The Gazette* in 1972. He has produced 31 books, either collections of his own work or books that he has illustrated. The recipient of two National Newspaper Awards and five individual prizes from The International Salon of Caricature, in 1985 Mosher became the youngest person ever to be inducted into The Canadian News Hall of Fame.

aislin@globale.net

www.aislin.com
www.southam.com/montrealgazette
www.cagle.com

"BE SENSIBLE," YOU SAY? I'M TIRED OF BEING SENSIBLE! LAST YEAR, MY OWN GRANDSON MADE 468% ON SOMETHING CALLED ratsass.com!

Born in 1952 in South Africa, DAVID ANDERSON (**ANDY**) worked for several newspapers in that country. He was the cartoonist for *The Rand Daily Mail* until its closure in 1985 and then for *The Johannesburg Star*. Freelancing in Toronto since 1990, he still e-mails two editorial cartoons a week back to the *Star*.

ANYONE HAVE AN IDEA ON HOW TO TURN THIS Y2K THING INTO AN ANNUAL EVENT?

BADO is GUY BADEAUX's last name pronounced phonetically. Born in Montreal in 1949, he worked there for ten years before moving to Ottawa in 1981 to become the editorial page cartoonist for *Le Droit*. Author of 6 collections of his own work, he served as first president of the Association of Canadian Editorial Cartoonists and won the 1991 National Newspaper Award.

bado@ledroit.com

www.ledroit.com
www.artizans.com
www.art.vianet.fr/presse/
www.cagle.com

Le modèle québécois

Born in Montreal in 1945 and having studied painting and graphic arts at l'École des Beaux-Arts, **SERGE CHAPLEAU** became an instant celebrity in Quebec in 1972 with a weekly full colour caricature for *Perspectives*. He joined *Montreal Matin* two years later, where he did editorial cartoons until the paper folded following a long strike. Serge resurfaced at the very sedate *Le Devoir* in the mid eighties and has been at *La Presse* since April 1996. He won the National Newspaper Award for Editorial Cartooning in 1998 and 1999.

serge.chapleau@lapresse.ca

GARY CLEMENT was born in Toronto in 1959. Over the last ten years his illustrations have appeared in *The New York Times*, *The Wall St. Journal*, *The Boston Globe*, *The Globe & Mail*, *The Financial Post*, *The Washington Post*, *The Medical Post* and several other Posts. He has also written and illustrated two children's books: *Just Stay Put* (Fall 96) and *The Great Poochini* (Fall 99), which won the Governor General's Award for illustration. Winner of four National Magazine Awards as well as awards from the Advertising & Design Club of Canada, *Applied Arts* magazine, American Illustration and The American Society of Newspaper Design. He lives in Toronto with his wife, two kids and various members of the animal kingdom.

gclement@nationalpost.com
www.nationalpost.com
www.cagle.com

Born in Toronto in 1951, **PATRICK CORRIGAN** studied fine arts at the Ontario College of Art, which led to a career of night-shift taxi driving. He forsook his extensive art training and freelanced for *The Financial Post*, *Maclean's* and *The Toronto Star*. He joined the *Star* in 1983 as a full-time illustrator, while filling in for Duncan Macpherson whenever possible. Twice nominated for a National Newspaper Award he has won several awards in illustration and graphics (Society of Newspaper Design, New York Art Directors Club, Advertising Design Club of Canada, Toronto Art Directors Club). He was named the editorial page cartoonist in 1995 at *The Toronto Star* and can still quote you a return fare from the airport.

corrigan@thestar.ca
www.thestar.com
www.cagle.com

ANDRÉ-PHILIPPE COTÉ, born in 1955, has been the editorial cartoonist of *Le Soleil* since the summer of 1997. Author of the comic strip "Baptiste" (since 1984), he has also worked for the humour magazine *Safarir* in the last decade. He has published nine books so far.

www.lesoleil.com
www.art.vianet.fr/presse/

Born in Alberta in 1965, **CRAIG GEORGE** is a freelance cartoonist based out of Calgary. His editorial cartoons have been featured in numerous daily newspapers across the country (*The Calgary Herald, The Calgary Sun, The Edmonton Journal,* the Regina *Leader-Post, The Toronto Sun, The Ottawa Citizen, The Globe and Mail*) and in over 30 weekly newspapers across the Western Provinces. The regular cartoonist for *The Western Producer*, he works and resides in suburbia with his wife, Julie, step-son, Nicholas, and his son, Benjamin.

Born in 1948 in St. Thomas, Ontario, **DALE CUMMINGS** studied animation and illustration at Sheridan College in Oakville. During a brief stay in New York he did some cartoons for *The New York Times*. He returned to Toronto in 1976, where he freelanced for *Last Post, Canadian Forum, Maclean's, The Toronto Star, Canadian Magazine* and *This Magazine*. Full-time editorial cartoonist with *The Winnipeg Free Press* since 1981, he won the National Newspaper Award in 1983.

www.artizans.com
www.cagle.com

MICHAEL DE ADDER works out of Halifax as a regular contributor to *The Chronicle Herald/Mail Star,* the Saint John *Times Globe* and *Coast* magazine. He also works as the chief editorial cartoonist at *The Hill Times* in Ottawa. His main endeavour is illustrating a daily political cartoon strip called *Cabinet Shuffles,* which appears in several newspapers across Canada. De Adder originally hails from New Brunswick and obtained a Bachelor of Fine Arts degree from Mount Allison University in 1991.

deadder@hfxnews.southam.ca

TIM DOLIGHAN was born in 1966 and lives with his wife Mary and daughters Caili and Shanna in Orono, Ont. After receiving degrees from Laurier, York and Ottawa U (none of which had anything to do with art), he started freelancing and illustrating for community newspapers in 1992. He has received several community newspaper awards and is currently published in over 50 papers across Canada including the Montreal *Gazette, The Toronto Sun* and various Metroland papers.

dolighan@home.com

ANDY DONATO was born in Scarborough in 1937. He graduated from Danforth Technical School in 1955 and worked at Eaton's as a layout artist. He joined the Toronto *Telegram* in 1961 as a graphic artist working in the promotion department. In 1968 he was appointed art director and began cartooning on a part-time basis. After the demise of the *Telegram,* he joined *The Toronto Sun* and in 1974 started cartooning on a full-time basis. In 1985-86 he served as president of the Association of American Editorial Cartoonists.

www.canoe.com/TorontoSun/donato.html
www.cagle.com

DUŠAN PETRIČIĆ was born in Belgrade, Yugoslavia, in 1946. He graduated from Belgrade's Academy for Applied Arts, where he also taught illustration. Editorial cartoonist for the daily *Večernje Novosti* (Evening News) and the weekly magazine *Nin*, Petričić is the author of numerous children's books and has directed many animated films. He has won several awards: Grand Prix in Tokyo, Silver medal in Istanbul, Grand Prix in Skopje, and Golden Pen in Amsterdam. In Canada since September 1993, he has had cartoons published regularly in *The Toronto Star* and the book review section of *The New York Times*.

www.thestar.com
www.artizans.com

JOHN FEWINGS was born in Simcoe, Ontario in 1955. He began drawing caricatures of his high school teachers to piss them off and get laughs from his friends; it worked on both counts. His first editorial cartoons appeared in *The Port Dover Maple Leaf* and *The Simcoe Reformer*. He now resides in Peterborough with Gale, Josh and their border collie Buddy, working as a freelance graphic designer/cartoonist. His cartoons regularly appear in the *Peterborough Examiner* and *The Toronto Sun*.

jfewings@sympatico.ca

Born in 1949 in Saskatoon, **BRIAN GABLE** studied fine arts at the University of Saskatchewan. Graduating with a B.Ed. from the University of Toronto in 1971, he taught art in Brockville and began freelancing for the Brockville *Recorder and Times* in 1977. In 1980 he started full-time with the Regina *Leader-Post* and is presently the editorial cartoonist for *The Globe and Mail*. He has won National Newspaper Awards in 1986 and 1995.

http://www./globeandmail.ca
http://www.cagle.com

150.

Born in Montreal in 1951, and after studies having nothing to do with drawing, MICHEL GARNEAU (**GARNOTTE**) has contributed to many newspapers and magazines in Montreal, including *CROC*, *TV Hebdo*, *Protégez-vous (Protect Yourself)*, *Titanic* (of which he was editor-in-chief), *Les Expos*, *Je me petit-débrouille*, *La Terre de chez nous* and *Nouvelles CSN*. He became the editorial cartoonist for *Le Devoir* in April 1996.

garnotte@ledevoir.ca

www.ledevoir.com

Born in Montreal in 1964, **ÉRIC GODIN** is an illustrator, graphic artist, painter and produces, since september 1999, a daily cartoon for the TVA television network called "Le petit dessin de Godin". For 30 seconds, viewers see, to the accompaniment of a jazz tune, a cartoon being drawn in front of their eyes. He was the first daily online cartoonist in Quebec and worked, for 11 years, at *Voir*, a Montreal weekly.

MIKE GRASTON was born and raised in Montreal. He has been editorial cartoonist with the *Windsor Star* since 1980, after having spent time obtaining an honours degree in history from the University of Western Ontario and freelancing for the *Ottawa Citizen*. His work has appeared in most Canadian newspapers as well as a number of American publications and has been featured on ABC's Nightline, CBC, CTV and CBC Newsworld. He has three daughters: Lisa, Carly and Rachel.

graston@home.com

www.southam.com/windsorstar

.151

Born in Liverpool, **GRAHAM HARROP** emigrated to Canada at the constant urging of friends, family and the British Government. He has worked in a mill, a paint store and once drove cab in a gorilla suit. He draws *Back Bench* and was hired by *The Vancouver Sun* in an attempt to get him to renew his subscription. (It worked.)

www.artizans.com

Here boy... taste the nice barbeque sauce on my finger!

DUNCES WITH WOLVES.

W.A. **BILL HOGAN** was born in Montreal, but has spent most of his life in Miramichi, New Brunswick. He presently does weekly cartoons for *The Miramichi Leader*, *Miramichi Weekend* and *Campbellton Tribune*, and freelances across Canada. Winner of numerous Atlantic community newspaper awards and the 1994 Atlantic Journalism Award for editorial cartooning, he has published three collections of his cartoons.

How will we know if we've cut too deep?
Try to get re-elected!

ROAD BUILDERS • ROAD TOLLS • AGRICULTURE • CIVIL SERVICE

BERNARD SISSORHANDS

JÉ (Charles Jaffé) was born in 1952, in Toronto. He spent several years at a boarding school in England where he encountered the cartoons of *Punch* and the *New Yorker*. His own cartoons have been published in *The Spectator*, *The Oldie* and *Schlagzeilen* in Europe and regularly in *The Women's Quarterly* in the States. In Canada, his work is tolerated in *Frank*, *The Law Times* and *Solid Waste & Recycling Magazine*. He has been fired from more daily newspapers than he has been a cartoonist for, is presently trying to be normal and is freelancing as a charming, efficient, courteous, inexpensive illustrator with no political views whatsoever.

www.sentex.net/~cjaffe

"Look dear! His first hostile take-over bid!"

152.

ANTHONY JENKINS was born in Toronto and spent his early career delivering *The Globe and Mail*. He joined the paper in 1974. In the 1980s he took three year-long leaves of absence to travel in 74 countries. During the 1980s, he also began writing for the paper and continues today as a regular contributor. He draws the "J" cartoon at the *Globe* and still lives in Toronto with two daughters.

www./globeandmail.ca

Born in 1965, **PAUL LACHINE** lives in Chatham, Ontario, with his wife Deborah and their children Katie and Michael. His freelance editorial cartoons and illustrations appear in 20 dailies across Canada and the United States, including *The London Free Press*, *The Ottawa Citizen*, *The Vancouver Sun*, *The Chicago Tribune*, *The San Francisco Times Chronicle* and *The Washington Post*. When not cartooning, he is busy brainwashing his children into becoming rabid Montreal Canadiens fans.

Born in Swift Current, Saskatchewan, in 1950, **JOHN LARTER** started at *The Lethbridge Herald* in 1974 and went to *The Edmonton Sun* in 1978. He was *The Toronto Star's* editorial cartoonist from 1980 until he returned west in 1989 to take the same position at *The Calgary Sun*.

www.canoe.com/CalgarySun/larter.html
www.artizans.com
www.cagle.com

ROBERT **LEA** is a freelance cartoonist who survives as a graphic artist in Moncton, N.B.

Born in Kitchener, Ontario, in 1964, **JACK LEFCOURT** graduated with a B.A. in fine arts from the University of Waterloo. He started cartooning for the university student paper syndicate in 1985 and has been drawing professionally since 1988. His work is published in about 20 dailies and weeklies across Canada and he is currently the regular editorial cartoonist for *NOW* in Toronto.

www.lefcourtland.com

GARETH **LIND**, 36, has been cartooning for almost as long as he can remember. His political and social satire strip, *Weltschmerz*, appears in Toronto's *eye* weekly, the Ottawa *X Press* and other Ontario weeklies. An additional cartoon appears nationally in the bi-monthly *This Magazine*. Lind is based in Guelph, Ontario, where he is self-employed as a graphic designer by day and a struggling cartoonist by night. He has been known to sleep on occasion.

lind@web.net

GRAEME MACKAY was born in Hamilton in 1968. After studying politics at the University of Ottawa, he flew off to England and sold bacon to famous people at a downtown London department store. When he nearly sliced his fingers off he returned to Hamilton where he freelanced political caricatures. In 1997, he landed a job as editorial cartoonist for the *Hamilton Spectator*.

gmackay@hamiltonspectator.com

www.geocities.com/GPee
www.geocities.com/gridlock_cartoon
www.cagle.com

BRUCE MACKINNON grew up in Antigonish, N.S., studied fine arts at Mount Allison University, and was a member of the Graphic Design program at the Nova Scotia College of Art and Design. He started doing a weekly editorial cartoon with *The Halifax Herald* in 1985, working at home while raising his newborn daughter, Robyn. Through the miracle of day-care, he was able to join the *Herald* on a full-time basis in August of 1986. He has won several Atlantic Journalism Awards for editorial cartooning, was named "journalist of the year" in 1991, and was the National Newspaper Award winner for both 1992 and 1993.

bpmack@ns.sympatico.ca

www.herald.ns.ca
www.artizans.com
www.cagle.com

MALCOLM MAYES was born in Edmonton in 1962. Editorial cartoonist for *The Edmonton Journal* since June 1986, his work has appeared in most major Canadian newspapers and many major American newspapers, as well as numerous books and magazines including *Best Editorial Cartoons of The Year* (USA), *Reader's Digest*, and *The Great Big Book of Canadian Humour*. In addition, his cartoons have been featured on CBC, CNN, and at Montreal's International Museum of Humour.

mmayes@artizans.com

www.artizans.com

MICHAEL F. EDDENDEN (ME) was born in Hamilton, has acquired degrees in anthropology and architecture and two kids along the way. His wife chose him. His comic strip *Between Polls* first appeared in *The Globe and Mail*. He currently appears weekly in *Marketing Magazine*.

eddenden@pathcom.com

THEO MOUDAKIS (MOU) was born in Montreal in 1965 where he began freelancing for *The Gazette* in 1986. In 1991 he started full-time with the *Halifax Daily News* and in September 2000 became editorial cartoonist for *The Toronto Star*. His work has appeared in most Canadian dailies as well as *The New York Times*, *Time* and *Mad*, and has been twice shortlisted for the National Newspaper Award.

www.thestar.com
www.artizans.com
www.cagle.com

DAN MURPHY was born in Missouri. He moved to Canada in the early seventies, drawing for various underground newspapers and aboveground magazines. He is a cartoonist and columnist for the Vancouver *Province*.

dmurphy@pacpress.southam.ca

www.artizans.com

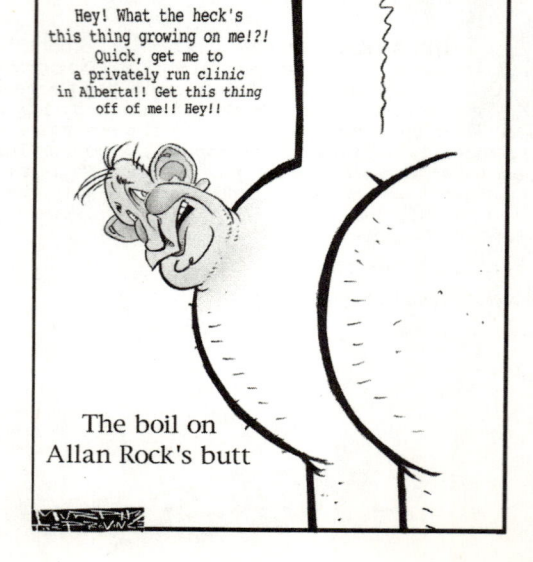

Born in 1955 in Woodbridge, Ontario, **STEVE NEASE** is art director of *The Oakville Beaver*, producing regular editorial cartoons and his family humour comic strip, *Pud*, which are both syndicated by Miller Features. Nease is a four-time recipient of the Canadian Community Newspapers Awards for cartooning. He and his wife Dian live in Oakville, and have four sons: Robert, Ben, Sam and Max.

snease1@home.com

Born in Winnipeg in 1936, **ROY PETERSON** works for *The Vancouver Sun* and *Maclean's*. His work has appeared in all major Canadian and most major American newspapers and magazines. He worked with Stanley Burke on the best-selling *Frog Fables & Beaver Tales* series and has illustrated many book covers and produced his own children's book, *The Canadian ABC Book*, as well as two collections of his cartoons: *The World According to Roy Peterson* and *Drawn & Quartered*. Married with five children, he was, in 1982-83, the first Canadian-born president of the Association of American Editorial Cartoonists. He won the Grand Prize at the International Salon of Caricature in Montreal in 1973 and is a seven-time winner of the National Newspaper Award.

www.cagle.com

INGRID RICE is a self-syndicated cartoonist published in over 50 markets across Canada and throughout B.C. Although she has not won any contests, she has appeared before the B.C. Press Council and been found to be reprehensible. Her free time is spent caring for assorted guinea pigs and a cat.

DAVE ROSEN was born in Montreal in 1955 and started out cartooning for the underground press at the age of 16. After freelancing for a number of years, he quit the field for a career in radio, and ultimately, stand-up comedy. While continuing his work as a broadcaster and comic, he returned to the drawing board in 1993 as editorial cartoonist for the alternative Montreal weekly *HOUR* and has been there ever since. He has published three books: *Megatoons, The Quebec Neverendum Colouring and Activity Book* and *What Happened?!*

toons@total.net

www.go.to/whathappened

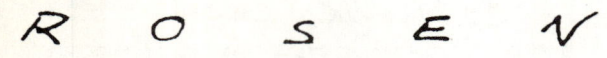

ROSEN

FRED SEBASTIAN was born (in 1964) and bred in Ottawa. A graduate of Algonquin College's Commercial Art/Graphic Design program, his work appears in *Legion, The Province* (Vancouver), *The Toronto Star, The National Post* and *The New York Times Book Review.* In 1994, he won a *Studio* magazine merit award for illustration.

sebastian@cyberus.ca

www.reuben.org/sebastian
www.cagle.com

SEBASTIAN

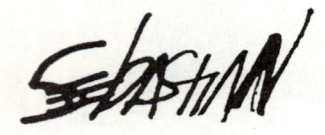

PHILIP STREET, was born in Blyth, Ontario in 1959. He studied English at the University of Toronto and, much later, animation at Sheridan College. His comic strip *Fisher* has appeared in *The Globe and Mail* since 1992. He lives in Toronto with his wife, Vanessa Grant.

pstreet@interlog.com

PHILIP STREET

Born in London, England, in 1926, **BEN WICKS** claimed to have held the Nazis at bay during the war as a swimming pool attendant at a Canterbury army camp. Having learned to play the saxophone in the army, he toured Europe with a band and was later to play in the orchestra on the liner *Queen Elizabeth*. Wicks moved to Canada in 1957, working as a milkman in Calgary. He sold several gag cartoons to *The Saturday Evening Post* and never looked back. Moving to Toronto in 1960, he produced a daily syndicated cartoon, *Wicks*, and was named to the Order of Canada in 1986. He died on September 10, 2000.

— Don't blame me. Blame Health Canada and their cut backs.

VINCENT WICKS was born in Calgary in 1959. Leaving school at 18 and traveling through South and Central America before settling down in Canada to become a professional musician, he now draws the syndicated comic strip *The Outcasts*.

MICHAEL ZAHARUK was born in Toronto in 1965. After graduating from the Ontario College of Art in 1991, he began freelancing as an illustrator and political cartoonist. His work has appeared in such publications as *The Toronto Star*, *The Globe and Mail*, *NOW* magazine, the Guelph *Mercury*, *The Utne Reader* and other magazines across North America. Since 1994 he has been a regular contributor to Union Art Services, a co-operative mailing service distributing political cartoons and graphics.

IN ADDITION TO PORTFOOLIO, HERE IS A LIST OF RECENT EDITORIAL CARTOON COLLECTIONS:

AISLIN and Gordon Snell, *Yes! Even More Canadians!*, McArthur and Co.
BADO, *Salades du chef*, L'Interligne, Ottawa.
CHAPLEAU, *L'année Chapleau 2000*, Boréal, Montreal.
CÔTÉ, *De tous les...Côté 2000*, Le Soleil, Quebec.